Andrew 'MulletProof' Grav
regular face on the performan   ... on
6 Music's Cerys Matthews ʃnow and BBC Four's
documentary *Evidently John Cooper Clarke*, Andrew is
favoured by comic book legend Alan Moore, and has
been cited as *the hardest working poet in the East Midlands.*

Light

at the end of the

tenner

Andrew 'MulletProof' Graves

Burning Eye

This edition published by Burning Eye Books 2014

www.burningeye.co.uk

@burningeye

Burning Eye Books
15 West Hill, Portishead, BS20 6LG

ISBN 978 1 90913 6304

Cover design by Mark Dickson

CONTENTS

Truth

is like sex.
Everyone wants it,
it can leave you breathless, exhilarated
and can be bought on street corners.

Unlike sex however,
without truth,

you're fucked.

A Careless Voyeur

"Flashing blue lights, camera, action
watching my life, main attraction."

Richard Archer

Radford Road

A saffron dance
on a cloudless day
bounds across
a taxi bonnet,

forms a
swirling sari love,
written in a
red brick sonnet

for incense burning
Naan bread ovens
sweating, promised
spiced meat holes,

patois Sunday
chances lost,
for hair-weave girls
and mouths of gold.

Burkas mix
with tracksuit gobs
and kids on scooters
learn to fly

past tram stops
and each paper shop,
curbs of
random paradise.

Tandoor sunset
frames the day,
dark window movie
presentations,

trailers for a
fruit stall magic,
circus colouring
ripe sensations.

A parade of citrus,
white teeth smiles,
in themes of
burst kaleidoscope,

to moments kept
in slot machines
tied with bits of
skipping rope.

In a market where
stretched canvas wraps
the bartering soliloquy,

a disused pub for
money changers,
knock-off jeans
and hosiery.

Crossings
are for decoration,
piano keys
for cars to play,

traffic lights are
incidental,
lanterns for the
come what may.

Shadows slip into
the cracks
dusk falls onto
road's warm skin,

a cinnamon
dusted candy neon,

place to keep your spirit in.

Leftover

Can you let me out, love?
she asks,
counting dad's money.

Her face, a beautiful hatchet job,
whiplash mascara
bleeds apologies
into gin and tonic skin,
coat of cigarette burns, market PVC.

Before I close the door
I watch barely black legs
disappear.

The tell-tale laddered,
middle aged wiggle

only makes me sad.

15, I'm lost

in perfume

that won't let go.

The Love Tree

A tree waits up by the estate,

longs for regal forest
of fantasy,
Rupert Bear annuals
or Enid Blyton innocence,

instead gets
dog-shit laden
paths of gob,
broken beer-can,
Durex bushes,

a Neverland jungle
of bleeding wildlife
battles,
where weeds
are sprayed with piss
and fairies dare not
dance.

A tree waits up by the estate.

Then one day

a crude heart
is carved into
its moss green skin,
a joyous scar
formed
in the post coital
mess of ring pull proposal,

when its bark became
a wedding bed,
to sap bursting
bride and groom,
honeymoon damp kisses,

before their long walk home.

A tree waits up by the estate,

pulse found,
leafy fingers stretch out
in morning after bliss,

emerald aerials reach
for sky torn freedoms,
rooftop romance
and council house love,
transcending telegraph poles,
abandoning the back streets
and bullet ridden boulevards,

longing now gone,
roots alive with creeping faith.

A tree waits up by the estate.

A tree wakes up by the estate.

Daze

Between days of baggy-arse smoulder
and realms of Gallagher scallywag rolls,
mediocrity sucker punch blows
before The Jam had T-shirts in Tesco,

came second hand Saturday record shop pride
fleabag, charity discs in the dust,
scratchy persuasions of gatefolding pleasures
black plastic moments to make the world just.

The mix tape meandering sad song collection,
nursing of a heartache's unplaced kiss.
The Cure's Sunday morning dark twisted ballads
drawn curtain promising, long playing bliss

lyric sheet lingering candle cold rooms
blu-tacking posters to peeling damp walls,
twelve inch reprisals to all that life offered
rent cheques for B sides and a kick in the balls.

Rammel Nitrate: Nottinghamshire Kisses and Laced History Lessons

An earthquake wakes
the sleeping city,
blood runs through
its sandstone veins,
slashed with tramline
scars that burn
on bones of splintered
stocking frames.

A prehistoric
cave tattooed
in scabs of bitter
miners' strikes,
riding revolutions home
on steeds of
rusting *Raleigh* bikes

to market towns
of civil war,
ancient pint pot
holy grails,
Salvation Army
lanes that flood
with bubbling fonts
of *Shipstone's Ale*

to churchyards where
Lord Byron creeps
on needle tracks
and cobbled paths
spun with spider
webs of lace
that decorate
an aftermath

of dug up worlds
and tunnels weaved
through JM Barrie's
pirate tale,
where arboretum
daydreams blur,
with lost boy spells
on hangman trails.

On streets where books
have learned to drink
to ghosts of Sillitoe
under dogs
who suffer torments
of the damned
and sickly
DH Lawrence snogs.

Where Hitchcock crashing
Jimmy Stewart
falls to war wound's
Vertigo,
Clarke Gable's
Mansfield matinee
of ageing coaldust
picture shows.

Choking *John Player*
special smokes
fog the *Pretty Polly*
seams
that stalk around the
Broadway café's
gunshot silver
heartache screen.

A flickered history
music hall
applauding
old Fred Karno's wit
with silent laughter
custard pies
which splatter
every football kit

branded with each
tree of strength,
thieving magpie,
stripes of pain,
the black and white
of news reels brusied
by tackles in
the pouring rain,

which bounces off
each high rise flat
and *This is England*
closing scenes
to drown the noise
of Broadmarsh rows
and skateboard rolling
town hall teens.

In reimagined
Brighton Rocks
Where Pinky lurks
On Sherwood Rise,
a flick-knife in his
Paul Smith suit,
a lethal Bingo
mystery prize

by Ramadam roads
the castle flows,
with warming
Caribbean breeze
that builds into
a Goose Fair gale,
of steaming
mint sauced
mushy peas,

a food of love's
convenience
in sandwiches
of polish bread
crusts of counter
culture meals
in recipes
to feed
the heads

of every body
and Merry Man,
in hoods of casual
modesty
stained with henna
and shopfloor rust,
and skins of
cold sincerity.

Owls

They're just shapes at first
broad shadowed crucifix
half glimpsed distortions,
bat signals cast against
the city's failing light,

the parliament of owls resumes.

St Ann's summer incidents,
quick as trigger moments,
nocturnal feathered burglars
uncaptured by a mobile phone
unreported by the press,

the parliament of owls resumes.

Unhampered by democracy,
spurning random ballot box
for wing span evolution,
beak and talon testaments,
policies designed in
regurgitated skulls,

the parliament of owls resumes.

The War

Her face is later than night
older than the world,
her concerns go on forever
but she is given just a moment

by the policeman impatient
with her bags of value
groceries and dented cat food tins.

In the store behind them,
slick buzz cuts
in tight charcoal trousers

and crisp white shirts
haggle deals with customers
there for shelter
not handsets.

A child stops
by the coffee house window
his violet lips press
against the freezing glass,

mother,
busy adjusting a faulty strap
on cheap plastic shoes,
finally notices
and drags him away,
protests fade
but goodbye kisses linger.

Pigeons skulk
on rooftops
and leaky gutters relieve
themselves on beat up
pavements,
guilty with spit
and chewing gum stains

above everything
morose clouds form
alliances, their treaties signed
with jet plane trails

but the war goes on.

Wings

'Coo,' says the pigeon.
Somewhere above him
in the dank rafters of the
underpass that derelicts
sometimes use as a toilet.

Frank is back by the canal again,

a gale blows
thinning grey hair wisps
into lips, weather cracked
with unsaid words.

Icy rain seeps through
loose and tattered greatcoat,
pulled tight
around his awkward
ill balanced frame

pale eyes
watering with bitter cold
stare out across the city,
and he knows it for what it is:

blinking street-lamps lead to
arrogant, shoe shops
and slick over-lit supermarkets.

They bristle against
manic-depressive schoolyards
the neon gruel of takeaway lands

and aching, heart-broken tenements.

Red tail-lights bleed
into the distance,
forever open wounds.

A refugee in his own hometown.

He does a quick mental inventory
of his latest non-achievements.

1. Get lodger, who will stink out my house with foul
smelling foot odour, steal my belongings and fuck off
without paying me a penny in rent. (Tick)
2. Fall in love with her. Never talk to her. Instead admire
her from afar and wait till she eventually moves away
forever. (Tick)
3. Be a bad friend. Lose friends. Make new friends called
Jim Beam, *Jack Daniels* and *Johnny Walker*. (Tick)
4. Create mental inventory of recent failures and
misfortunes just to really stick the knife into myself. (Tick)
5. Become a mental stress time bomb. (Tick…tick…tick…)

Then he feels it
hit him in the face.

It's not rain this time.

It feels slightly warm.
He wipes it away,

looks to chapped, wrinkled
palm now covered
in greeny-white bird-shit.

Up above, the pigeon looks
down.

'Coo,' it says again.

The final indignation,

thinks Frank.

Even nature wants
to empty its load upon him.

He picks up a stone,
squints into the dark,

thinks about lobbing it
at the feathered criminal above.

Then, the bird hobbles into sight.
It leans out over the small
overhang caked in excrement
peers indifferently
into the murky water.

'Coo,' it says again.

One of its feet has been
partly eaten away by disease,
some of its plumage is missing,
exposing
painful looking wounds about its
semi-naked chest.

The pigeon realises
it's being watched,
looks beneath to Frank.

Its tiny head cocks to one side,
as if taking him in,
weighing up the
scruffy looking human

then it switches its gaze
to dense night above,

without warning
takes to the air,
      it travels awkwardly out across the canal,

                  seems surprised,
         as though only just remembering
                   what its wings
                      are for,

             it flies out ascending
               over the grimy,
              endless rooftops,
           TV aerial forests and
              spiderweb cables
                  Beyond.

   For a second it is caught
        In the halo of a distant orange street light…

    Then it is gone.

Frank feels the stone
drop from his fingers

watches it bounce
on the
ancient cobbles
before it plops
sadly into the
water.

As the ripples fade,

so does the anger.

As he walks home
through the storm,
despite the cold

he lets his ill fitting
greatcoat blow open,
the tattered material
flutters unfurled in
the battering,
skin tightening wind

the old man smiles,

though Frank cannot fly

he's found

his wings.

Rocket Fuel Tears

"No words to describe it. Poetry! They should've sent a poet. So beautiful. So beautiful... I had no idea."

From the film Contact (1997)

Astronomy

A *Special Brew* cadet
on nervous virgin flight

gets orbited by threats,
approaching voices in the night

bought down by the G Force
of a kitchen sink sci-fi

by angry young Jedi
flashing light-sabre flick knives,

launched into a nightmare
crashing hard against the soul

lost and adrift in
galaxies of hate,

mission now abandoned
head smashed against the grate

a bleeding constellation
organized in scars,

a dawn gutter tragedy
unnoticed by the stars.

Project Mercury: Liberty Bell 7
(For Gus and Betty)

When the hatch blew
you didn't need Shepard
with his gas station growl
to say you'd screwed the pooch old Gus,

yeah, Nixon must have pissed his pants
and while Glen was still all
Yankee Doodle Jesus
Betty knew it had all gone to shit.

She saw it in your eyes
it bubbled away
in the splashdown whiskeys
the fury and the fuck you prayers
and Jackie Kennedy's
non-existent smile.

You'd lost the Liberty Bell
to saltwater depths
weighed down with the wrong stuff
the Senate's heavy gaze and
panic button blues.

Red carpet copters sweeping over
oceans of embarrassment
could save a drowning spaceman
but pride was left for the fishes
and Star City laughter.

There would be no ticker-tape
or Whitehouse lunches
just locker room trials
test flight guilty secrets
and sonic booming silences,

official truth stuffed
deep into silver lining,
unwanted as the souvenirs
from a trip blown into heaven
that only crashed to hell,

and 7 years later
did you laugh Gus?
In those final few seconds of
white heat terror
hatch refusing to blow
stubborn as the science
that put you there,
redesigned for something

you

never

did

as you watched Chaffee and White
burn into history,
did you finally get your peace?
Your guilt-free trip to the stars?
No space craft required
just a photo at the back of a bar

and Betty's rocket fuel tears.

On July 21, 1961, pilot Gus Grissom became the second American in space, in his tiny ship The Liberty Bell 7. Upon re-entry though, the hatch blew too early and after a struggle in which poor Gus almost drowned, the craft was lost to the depths of the ocean. This led to years of debate in which many considered Gus to have panicked and opened the hatch himself. As a result the hatches of subsequent spacecraft were redesigned, making it impossible for astronauts to open them from inside. Tragically it was such a hatch that eventually killed Gus and his crew in a test mission in 1967, two years before Armstrong set foot on the moon.

Tsiolkovsky

(Getting the science fiction wrong)

from scarlet fever
schoolyards

soundless vision
impossible flights

handmade lab
trajectories

destined for never
changing nights

feathers in
the centrifuge

revolutions born
before a time

paltry blood smeared
science books

stained mechanic
blueprint mind

dizzying dreams
of the firmament

God's stairway
leaving threadbare days

in the shadow of
Lenin's grand design

processions lit
by rocket blaze

Before his death in 1935, Konstantin Tsiolkovsky had established himself as the grandfather of rocket science, not only did he write the theory of rocketry but also came up with the Formula for Aviation. In his low-tech backyard laboratory, amongst other things, he was able to prove theories of high-speed space travel, utilising a cobbled together centrifuge and a number of unfortunate chickens...

Vostok 1

(Yuri Losing the World)

they play a love song

its melody, no more real
than the flicker book geography
rolling out below

angling away

Siberia's shambling horrors
cannot reach me now

I tell them I feel fine
our scratchy converse
a wireless irritation
words embarrassed
by the dark between us

I am not fine

I am impossibility
a speeding obscenity,
God's bullet
wounding the sky

scabs of light form
across the void's
eternal skin

Northern hemisphere
bleeds away
into shrinking
blue pacific

Я могу видеть все

I

       can

             see

                    everything

         and America sleeps tonight

Apollo 8

A crackled lunar
Bible passage
rolls over
unfamiliar waves,
Tranquility Sea
of frozen acres
in alabaster
Christmas cards.

Crew share stuttered
awkward moments,
science choking
season's greetings,
Houston's nervous
blessings aired
in ratings grabbing
moon-washed blur.

Thrusters tune
to silent carols,
in shadowed Vegas
sequinned shows,
a firmament of spangled black
in hallelujah Elvis
fame.

Spaceman stardust,
autographs
are scrawled into
the atmosphere,
as a blasphemy
of Beatles songs
accompany
eternity.

World's image
squeezed between
the ads of
Coca-Cola cosmos kids,
who drink to fizzing cold war fuse
and Soviet vodka
bitterness,

to capsules caught in
spinning snaps,
satellite vista
strange designs,
but Earthrise
gleam through dark expanse
won't dim
South Asia's
Napalm flash.

On Christmas 1968, NASA spacecraft Apollo 8, became the first manned flight to orbit the moon. The televised grainy pictures of our only satellite proved to be an exciting American first, yet it was the still photographs released after touchdown, of our own planet peaking from behind the dark side of the moon, which proved to be perhaps the most memorable. 'Earthrise' is still an iconic and breathtaking image and who knows, at the time it maybe helped us to understand our fragility thus fuelling the many anti-Vietman war protests and general desire for peace that exploded back on earth.

Atomic Starfishing Test Bomb Blues

The blue-black dome
is strangled by light,
hot green persuasion,
uneasy beams,
midnight blooms
into nuclear truth.

Honolulu babies
burn, into space
with hard-on science bombs,
making war with stars
and native gods,
in satellite
fusing firework hell.

Lime cools to pink,
into fizzling
lemonade death parade,
explosion's last breath
choking gobs
of blood
across the summer sky

to a fallout applause
of shoulder slapping,
Yankee smiling
missile glow,
where bank cheques
line the silo homes
of dust cloud
shadowing
freedom lands.

Apollo 13 Haiku

Lovell nearly died,
his team almost lost to space,

but the film was good.

Sputnik II

(For Laika 'Little Curly')   •

She was never
coming back
to Nikita's kisses
or peasant shack

rocket dog romanced
into orbit hell
revolution rung
in Pavlov's bells
blasted away
soft warmth betrayed
Whitehouse bitching
Red Square parades

harnessed and sentenced
starved and baptised
cosmic cremation
ashes consigned
across a moment
and a million miles
loyalty burned up
in Korolev smiles

funeral rites
heart-monitor prayers
lost in the history
in Yuri's blinding glare
to cemetery skies
and lullabies

postage stamp blessings
and comrade goodbyes

Voskhod 2

(Alexi's off world arts)

In new worlds you can stagger
space walk Van Gogh painted views
explore galaxies of gold
in Jackson Pollock avenues

Dance to thundered heartbeat
on tense umbilical cord
rest your eyes upon the always
a silvering cosmic lord

Float in cold make-believe
hurl cosmonaut grenades
decorate every space ship
with abstract angel shades

Watch meaning peel off time
melted by the rockets
forget hard rain reality
of existence and mock it

Keep each troubled dream at bay
cast surreal reflections
be silhouette caught technology
Soviet proud selection

Screen print your great escape
make impressionist spells
erase those freezing madhouse walls
starving bodies in Gulag cells

Forget galleries of scars
fall asunder clash together
burn a path to freedom
stride your way into forever

<

On 18th March 1965, Cosmonaut Alexi Leonov became the first human being to undertake a 'space walk'. Tethered only with the ship's umbilical cord he was able to 'walk' alone in space some 500 kilometres above the surface of the earth, quipping that 'the world really is round' to his astounded space crew. Alexi, coming from the chilly hardships of a Siberian background is also an accomplished artist and has captured his exploits in space on canvas many times over.

>

Following his momentous trip to the stars, Yuri Gagarin, the world's first space man was sent on a publicity tour of the UK. The Soviets were keen to highlight his workingman's credentials, he was an ex-foundry worker after all, so on the 12th July 1961 the cosmonaut arrived at the packed Metropolitan Vickers factory (Metros), Trafford Park, Manchester, to greet the eager workforce.

The Metropolitan Vickers Factory was bought out by GEC in 1967.

Gagarin died in a tragic plane crash during a routine training exercise on March 27th 1968.

Factory Space

Through moss side
via the stratosphere,
mobbed cosmonaut
orbits the Metro works,
listens to sharp northern prayers
for a traveller come home.

Incandescent specs
light the dark womb
of the foundry,
fading stars for the workers,
who're outside shaking hands
with their kind of rocket man.

Brush against Emerald uniform
perform mock-Kruschev
salutes
and marvel at god-like
peasant smiles
from one who's seen it all.

50 years on
at the closed factory gates
the town mourns
its strange VIP
with space ship serenades
and welded farewells,

weeps for his loss
now its own.

Finding Something to Lose

"Our dead are never dead to us until
we have forgotten them."

George Eliot

Nottingham Rock City, Saturday (Alternative Night) 1992

Here's a church of dredlocked glory,
tribal ink skinned, UB40s,
holy scratched discs, worshiped gods
snake hip freaks and weird sods,
see hormones clash with reverie
sick stains and the bon ami.

A violin-vexed tabernacle
celtic rune scored witch's cackle,
a thronging worshipped sweat brigade
of karma sliced with razor blades.
A midnight service, naked hymn,
white powder prayers on toilet rim.

See pulpit bleached-up preachers sing
of anarchy and far off things
to drum beats that will raise the dead,
Fuzzbox tunes to wake your head,
for angels decked in para boots,
damaged choirs and wrecked recruits.

Watch stripy-stockinged nuns look out
for t-shirt branded souls in doubt.
Heroines soaked in holy water
are crustie, folkey jangled daughters,
they glow in neon nightclub pale
leave snuck in vodka, fag ash trails.

It's a city centre sanctuary
for Eldritch zombie missionaries,
red lipped, late night fishnet boys
velvet speeding bondage toys,
dark apostle dance-floor snogs
sacrificed to dry ice fog.

Noises

Salutes of midnight
thunder glory,
a sphincter quiets
the chattering class
with a talent learned
in army barracks,
hysterical Paris
has found its son.

Controlling mobs
with raised
white finger
Joseph blows
a hurricane
it flows through palace
and run down house
unprejudiced
and odour free.

Copycats spoil
the toilet humour
court case rattles
the backstage door,
pantomime public
galleries,
in Moulin Rouge
smeared days ahead.

Retirement cracks
and accidents
stain skid marked
night's embarrassment,
the war kills Pujol's
cannon fire,

no smiles in stinking
trench latrines

M. Joseph Pujol (1857–1945) maintained unusual skills in abdominal muscle control, which made it possible for him to seemingly fart at will (in fact he did not pass intestinal gas, he was merely able to shift air into his bowels). Nevertheless, his anal impressions earned him fame fortune and even the attention of royalty. He was also one of the world's first recording artists. Amongst his 'impressions' was his very own 21-gun salute. He retired at the commencement of World War One, presumably drowned out by the sound of real bombs.

I Want My Money Back Jim Morrison

A black leather baritone
the Lizard King,
acid killing shaman,
lord of dark things.

Through doors
of perception
into desert dreams,
you cast light
on shadows, hid in beams.

Read our thoughts
through the back
of our minds,
gave us times
instead

of
        time

and we followed you
down every path

from the Whisky a Go-Go

to Paris bath.

Thanks

For the bread spread too thickly
with bright yellow butter,
brown chips that no one else
could make.

Your proper man's smell
and for not always taking
mam's side, 'cos she left anyway.

For that broad toothless grin in
beetroot bald head, for wearing
the same cardigan in
winter and *that* vest in July.

For being too wide for an
old armchair but never big
enough for the world.

For your services to football,
for taking the pledge
and for never letting me forget
that on that Sunday,

I was crying granddad,
not laughing.

Davy Jones

You were part of my Harold Lloyd teatimes
Champion The Wonder Horse,

summer holiday schemes

a daydream believing,
Last train to Clarksville
Manc' in

dream machine

cartoon performer maraca dance diva
psychedelic monkey
doing it

for the kids

never *Sleepy Jean* or
homeward queen
just a cheeky

back street prince

and it seems good times must start and end
say goodbye to our

smiling hipster lead

you may not have been in The Beatles baby
just the only boy band

I'd want or need.

Business Hours

Back to back bargains,
smashed city bomb nights
into bicycle journeying
retail flights
from *Metal Box* mishaps
machine laceration
book keeping promises
of quiet compensation.

Ukraine hands
laced with old country scars
embrace time in a carriage
under penny pinched stars
wired up to coal-dust
industrial scheming
redundancy love,
forging new life screaming.

Holding court in the shop
under lampshade recession
searching for custom
community blessings,
meeting awkward years
and prejudiced pain
through barricades of
work and crossed garden canes.

Foreign trips for grandkids
oven warm pies
and a royal line of moggies
betray hard to read eyes.

Here's to

Boxing Day scones
proper old photographs
welcome Sunday dinners

and an echo of that laugh.

Afterglow

A peacock with his bag of toys,
cockney sneering wall of noise,

all too beautiful, acid trips,
shitting cool on *YouTube* clips

a one man paisley-poncing scene,
pounding, wound up mod's young dream,

Tin Soldier issued feathercut,
low slung, punch bag to the gut.

In scissor kicks and monochrome breaks
blazing out to *Nut Gone Flake*

in arguments of flights on course
drunken, fiery song remorse,

an air raid sleazy psychedelic,
burning urchin bad arse relic

Gretsch feeds back in medley crashed

to encores formed in lyrical ash.

*Steve Marriott, lead singer, guitarist and main writer for 60s
mod legends The Small Faces, was arguably the coolest rock star
ever to have swaggered onto stage. His diminutive frame and
cockney urchin demeanour only seemed to enhance his innate*

grasp of entertainment and skilful songwriting. Marriott left us with timeless tunes such as All or Nothing and Tin Soldier, when he died in a house fire in 1991. The fire-fighter that discovered his body was coincidentally a big fan and perhaps summed the situation up for us all when he said, "It was like seeing part of our lives gone forever."

Hollywood Creeps and Monochrome

"… a place where they'll pay you a thousand dollars for a kiss and fifty cents for your soul."

Marilyn Monroe

QUADROPHENIA

Part 1:

Romantic

It's a lullaby sunset,
melody making,
heartache flung over
Brighton cliffs,
back alley dancing
fumbled duet, tyre-track
poem in a melting sand.
It's a parka shrouded,
unrequited, moment cast away,
to crashed *Lambretta's*,
fast goodbyes
and lovers drowning
in the rain.

Movies

We'll have no silk ribbons
tied to our words,
won't be sweetheart
stars of ten penny verse

sing no hymns
bound with awkward rhetoric,
when passion burns free
for love is a heretic

we'll not talk
of deep wounds bleeding,
pull petals from flowers
at flickering readings

won't pray to God
or be ashamed
of broken kisses
and souls unsaved

but we'll play our
record collections
get rained on in the park

and when the future leaves without us

watch movies

in the dark.

Hancock's Half-Baked Suicide

Stone me, what a life.
Is this it then?
The final few minutes
of a half hour
that's lasted over a decade.

I may as well be back at the Windmill,
those sticky fumblings of back row clientele,
half glimpsed through blinding
house-lights, nicotine choked curtains.

The backroom mauling showgirl jostle,
seamed stocking and whiplash parade.
Pitying eyes on those awkward feet,
shuffling hopeless into silence.

A belly full of jokes for that
ejaculate cathedral of button fly
penance and nudie show confessions.

Let he who is without sin
get the first round in…

Stone me.

An antipodean bow out lost
in the depth
of vodka practiced showmanship,
caught by rude awakenings
of a bastard chattering idiot box.

An audience of pills
and yesterday's dried breakfast.

The hotel keeps the world away
but bits keep creeping in.

All those smuggled bottles in Astrakhan,
intellectual delusions
and heavy browed excuses.

Echoed blood donor lines
vainly covering the stains
left by haemorrhaging
friends and co-stars.

Goodbye Kenny,

Bill,

Sid,

Hattie,

Ray and Alan…

Roll credits

Cue music…

At his prime Tony Hancock's radio shows alone could command audiences that would have the producers of today's X Factor signing Faustian pacts (though maybe they already have). His TV output was, initially, so popular that it was said he could empty pubs, such was the general public's hunger for his pompous persona. The fact that landlords lost so much custom when his TV programmes were on air proved to be ironic, considering that he became a depressive alcoholic in the last years of his life. His comedy life began with his run at the notorious London Windmill – a seedy strip club and training ground for nervous and up and coming comics. Over the years he systematically separated himself from a number of important contributors including Bill Kerr, Sid James, Kenneth Williams and even his writers Galton and Simpson. It was in Australia though, in the midst of recording a new series that he finally got rid of himself in an undignified suicide. The world said goodbye to perhaps the greatest comic turn that ever lived.

QUADROPHENIA

Part 2:

Lunatic

It's a tortured,
city scape, speeding vision,
pilled up, wanked off,
button down beast,
a petrol spilling, head collision
four-four beat
in a psycho ward.
It's Dr Jimmy's roundabout,
chaos skidding,
engine crunch,
a scooter straddling,
breakdown kiss,
tailor made for fashion punks.

Far From the Beach

A face much colder than a Christmas day,
prefab hands claw for stale welfare fates

search through rubble on brick dust blown sites
by old caravans on derelict nights

snot nose kiddie chorus, carbolic soap
hand me down daydreams form Reg's last hope

hers, lost coupons and scrubbed bleeding fingers
cursing cold skies, where no stars will linger

playing roulette fired with council house smiles
not just a night but a life on the tiles

gambled away, cast to life's waiting list
no two up two down...

...just morning choked mist.

On November 16th 1966, whilst swinging London did its thing and The Beach Boys ruled at number one, the BBC decided to show controversial drama Cathy Come Home. The play, about a young family who are made homeless and eventually have their children taken in to care, went on to be one of the most spoken of TV programmes in history. And whilst the film, when shown even now, retains enormous power, its director Ken Loach is perhaps sadly right when he claimed that it changed virtually nothing in terms of the housing problem. Recently statistics have shown that 8000 people in England alone are declared homeless each year but still denied access to services.

The Loneliness of a Long Distance Rumour

See that boy running,
world on fire in his chest,
a skinny kid defiant,
half cursed, half blessed.

He'll run from borstals
and dune snogging seasides,
from fresh girl wonders
and coppered up train rides,

from robberies designed
in dark angry blunders,
from dead dad realities,
prefabs and thunder,

from drainpipe confessions
where grey rains expose,
nicked hidden futures
and a lad on his toes

he'll run forever,
from factories and tumours,
chasing the whispers
of long distance rumours

from chimney stack Sundays
and rag and bone reasons
squeaking gate promises

and dole queue seasons.

*"If God is good, I will be able to play comedy.
And please God, may it be before I go screwy playing idiots,
half-wits and lunatics on the talking screen!"*

Dwight Frye

Dwight Frye (1899-1943) was without doubt, the scariest man the screen has ever seen. Forget Karloff and Lugosi (who Frye worked with on films like Frankenstein and Dracula), his particular brand of cackling bug eyed lunatic out does the lot (check out his portrayal of Renfield for starters). Sadly he was perhaps the most reluctant monster ever to appear too. His heart was actually in Broadway comedy, where he worked well for years. The studios had other ideas and saw him trapped as psychotic sidekick in a plethora of low budget horror flicks. His final indignity came after he died of a coronary, on a bus on the way back from the cinema, a bizarre oversight saw his death certificate give his occupation as Tool Designer. Being an old Vaudeville man, I hope he saw the joke.

Dead Man Walking

A Frankenstein experiment rots forever on the silver screen,
when shadows of ambition linger, in creepy crawling misery,
kept in fizzing diode prisons, typecast into tales of terror,
movie lonely lunatics

and cob web insecurities.

A career dug up in graveyard rains, fed insect husk indignity,
demoted to a monster's pet, smothered by Lugosi's cloak,
spotlights fall to fly chewed freak, Hollywood's Golden Age
is smeared, in unknown sidekick fingerprints

and spidery insanity.

A comedian trapped in phantom zone, cemetery laughs for
popcorn kids, Vaudeville villainous greasepaint stains the
        slapstick dancing funny man,
no Lazarus lightning conduit to resurrect a life gone wrong,
contract coffin nailed tight shut

with rusted possibility.

Tired of haunting, bat wing fluttering, stuttering worn down
        hideousness,
Gothic castle fortress locked with binding studio dungeon
        chains,
a bus ride lonely heart attack, creates mortuary embarrassment,
death certificate joke of jokes

in final script obscenity.

QUADROPHENIA

Part 3:

Tough Guy

It's a flick knife snickering,
bike chain boogie,
beach fight bleeding,
stab in the back,
it's a court case juvenile,
soul house swaggering,
broken shopfront,
split lip sneer,
a sick boy, blue dawn,
black eye thrilling,
sermonising brutal call,
fight club for the smart set kids,
and every *Sta-Prest* little thug.

Roles

The scene begins at night,
our shabby protagonist
waits by the taxi rank,
his rain slashed audience
all half cut chinos
and chip bag regrets,
provide a fee of
tossed pennies and acts of
random violence.
The X certificate picture,
projected onto screens
of urine spattered walls.

Hungry and Homeless,
thin, wobbly letters
scratched out in
stolen bookmaker's pen,
a hastily written script,
which sits
around his neck,

in the absence of words,
beneath the city's grinding
curse,
a fundamental subtitle
the world's too bored
to read.

Typecast in
surveillance movies,
harsh lights of
the chemist's glow,
directed by November

winds, lost in the upcoming
bleak double feature,
winter trailers and closed
down shelters,

no contracts signed
no sequel planned

but the story of
the street goes on…

"There is nothing there in the dark that isn't there when the lights are on"

Rod Serling

We're travelling through a dimension…

Where gun smoke meets with slick-black cool,
in charisma driven testament,
where wisdom crashes from the skies
on suburbs dark and paranoid.

Where softpack cigarette, deadline blues,
are wrapped in yellow fingered prose
a monochrome world of future shocks,
warnings bled through TV sets.

Where signposts point to episodes
trapped behind a dreamed up land,
pits of cancellation fears,
summits of the infinite.

Where tidal waves of sentiment
wash up hard reality,
corporate cold war fall out dust
and genie bottle messages.

Where concepts clash with killing fields,
Dallas shots and dirty dollars.
knickerbocker glory lies,
deep south water cannon riots

Where *Tupperware* sealed up picnic lives
are dragged from 50s vanity sleep
a blast disturbs America's dream
which wakes in Serling's *Twilight Zone*.

Creator and writer of the most original TV show to have ever come out of America – The Twilight Zone – Rod Serling was a true innovator, rebel, artist and campaigner. An old war veteran, using fantasy he helped slip issues like racism, tolerance and cultural understanding into prime time network television, despite strict censorship rules and sponsor clashes.

Candy Coating an Eternal Truth...

Like his more famous brother Willy,
Fred Wonka had a factory too...

A vegetable processing plant,
it sat alone on the hill,
overlooking the small but busy town.

People from miles around
failed to be in awe
of the distinctly un-magical place.

Not a single soul,
not even the most curious child
ever bothered to seek it out.

Fred, though, undeterred, tried emulating his brother
at every turn.

Where Willy had a
chocolate river and waterfall
Fred installed his own lake
of turnip juice, replete with
cabbage water fountain.

Where Willy had a sweet
and delectable candy
flavoured, edible playground,

Fred introduced his own,
laden with broccoli pieces
slowly browning pea pods
slithery carrot peelings
and pulped, mouldy onions.

And where Willy had Umpa Lumpas,

Fred employed hollow faced
wrecks from a
local job creation scheme.

He even tried marketing his own
Scrumdiddliumptious parsnips,
marvellous mushrooms
and ever lasting asparagus,

all to no avail.

It was a disaster.

One day, bored with all
the attention he wasn't getting,
despite the ingenious outfit he'd
knocked up from the insides of old
broad bean pods,
he decided he needed to take action.

Fred decided he would
hold his own competition.

Like his brother he would award
5 lucky children the chance to
visit the much not talked about place.

But when the fateful day came
and he threw open
those rusty and unimpressive
iron gates to the public,

unleashing the stomach churning
reek of putrefying spring greens,

the winners of the golden tickets,
which had been stapled haphazardly onto

randomly chosen florets of cauliflower,

never even bothered to turn up.

Heart broken he closed the factory come church come
financial disaster, and never opened it again.

But when the court case involving his brother
came up and the charges, including
driving a glass elevator
without due care or attention,
flagrant disregard of health and safety laws
and the physical abuse of minors, were read out…

suddenly Fred's problems
didn't seem so bad.

And when Willy was locked away the chocolate factory
was burned down
by a rabble of angry town's folk, who'd heard he must be a
paedophile.

Fred did his best to conceal the subtlest of smiles,

'Sweet,' he whispered to himself.

QUADROPHENIA

Part 4:

Hypocrite

It's a fading target
crossfire shot
nostalgia bait for
un-rode lives.
It's a t shirt
you can buy in *Next*,
logo for the fat and old.
It's a cranking world
of practiced pride,
breast fed raging, feather cut fake
a knackered patch
stitched to the soul,
rusting wheel at seasides lost.

Atomic Truths

*"Truth is like the sun. You can shut it out for a time,
but it ain't goin' away."*

Elvis Presley

Local

1.

The old boys'
wooden corner of history
is a malady of dominoes
and half recalled

Jamaican anecdotes,
distant trinkets,
in memories embellished,
slowly brewed deep within,

like the settling
Guinness pots before them.
Timelines reduced
to cold wet circles

on carved up tables,
the knock, knock acquiesce
of coconut sunshine,
childhoods gone.

BEAST

(Dedicated to Leftlion magazine – the one true voice of
Nottingham people)

Born out of the boredom
of the Viccy Centre void

a growling new creation
smiles and licks its claws.

Crawling from the afterbirth
of Kyle's lost generation

a Cloughie terrace cry
against the bullshit federation.

A mag on a mission
stalks its slab square manor

a takeaway stained flag
un-spangled banner.

An Arthur Seaton snog,
real ale smack to the lips,

a cat with combed mane,
guitar and snake-hips.

A Shane Meadows framing
antidote to fame,

a jamming session fuck you all
animal in the rain.

A back alley party,
fist fight on the street,

art-house philandering
lonely piece of meat.

A love poem spat
to the wrecks in the city,

press pack for the drifters
derelicts and un-pretty.

A slang prayer manifesto
slurred from every closed down pub,

a centerfold salute
to every struggling club.

A fanzine for the feckless,
dreamers and possessed,

a roaring bastard child

in a battle to the death.

Slash Seat Affair

An affair with Weller starts
with Brit pop summer streaming,
stripped down rattle dreaming,
Style Council meetings,
a distant pumping Jam bass lick.

An affair with Weller struts,
in vintage vestal moments,
dandy smart and lean keen,
for cool eyed threads and truth.

An affair with Weller sparks
with working class refusals,
peacock suited sonic kicks,
post-punk recitals,
classic urban psalms.

An affair with Weller blossoms
into full blown outdoor visions,
dripping *Wildwood* dusk,
losing time in tailored patterns,
of sunflower, serenaded fields.

An affair with Weller grows
in not so tranquil solitude, against
a raging noise of in-crowd fire,
a ragged feedback, broken riff ,
of changing men and love song soul.

Local

2.

The purveyor
of the out of reach,
sports bag guilty pleasures,
misspelled vodka labels

and never heard of fags,
lingers by the fruit machine,
waits for the landlord
to shout time

or God to call it a day,
lit by golden bells
of angels,
chorused by

last order chatter,
drained pint
empty payouts and
handpull prize decisions.

Games

The gentrification of
the human spirit goes on,
yet the two up three down,
laminated thinking,
plush exteriors of

the posh bit estates
won't hide the rot or
glorifications
of graveyard policy
parading through the streets

past protests we
can't have anymore,
the barbed wire bouquet
of the anti-truth brigade,
tabloid testaments

of slobbering disease,
paedophilic protestations of
barely legal page three spreads,
family values

and *Lego*

for the kids.

Jeremy Clarkson Just Fuck Off

It's only four wheels
and a roof,
a vehicle and not the truth,
you can't caress an oil stain,
or fall in love with a traffic lane,
or snog a sump or an MOT,
or snuggle with a parking fee.

A glove compartment holds no cheer,
you can't laugh, with knackered gears.
You'll never see a *Vauxhall* smile
in a million, million, million miles,
a car won't give you what you need,
a car will bring you to your knees.

A car is money and petrol smell,
combustion engine motor hell,
traffic jamming dents and prangs,
insurance cons and joy ride gangs,
a car might get you there, real quick

but a car cannot extend your dick.

Now the Deer Have Bought Kalashnikovs…

…there'll be no army surplus boots
no red check flannel peeking

from camouflage fatigues
no bourbon bodies breathless

in the quiet undergrowth
no exaggerated claims

of sexual liaisons to cheapen
the pine's great modesty

no cigarette stubs or mocking
laughter, just the humourless

work of the everglade's unseen
business, no stink of stale beer,

crushed can decorations
and cheap Davy Crockett hats

no more roof rack mortuaries
or tailgate processions

just the sun shot green canopy
and the assurance of a fair fight…

Local

3.

Over there
the familiar candy man,
umbilically attached
to outdoor public phone,

jots down whispered
new addresses,
between talk sexy cards
and fading taxi numbers.

His afterbirth
of chemical promise,
voodoo junkie,
pockets of ambition

are offered to
student naïve causes,
the shameless
bravado of idiot chaos,

his skittering, easy sales
technique, a sealed up
well-versed
alley way show.

Leaving

Wait!
Called the unicorn,
as the ark moved away
from the shore.

It began to rain again.

It's No Longer Tomorrow Yet...

She turns up
on a horse of rags,

in fields of fanfare chandeliers,
while skinless dogs of

glass look
back on lands of

night-time rainbow   thieves.

She leaps into a TV sky,

filled with plastic   glockenspiels,

concrete

waterfalls of green,

stitched in   worm-cast

tapestry

She dances on a piano
train, teaches

fruit flies how to drink
liquor made with Napalm jokes,

steam and cups of Mr Sheen

Down daisy toilet bowls

of time, she glides into a tourniquet,
swims in pools of skin and bone,

fuse wire
          dangled

                    ricochets.

Coaldust Mascara

I was wilfully strapped in straitjacket pains,
black leather, make-up, crashed crazy trains,

victim to bloodbath, baby doll ghouls,
Alice Cooper's brand of apocalypse cool.

You were held tight by emphysema days,
life-crushing breathless, tunnel vision haze

flying pickets, police, hissed scab remarks,
a small town's cruel war in the dark.

The space we shared, each room another land,
barricaded regions of choked up door slams,

my place of posters, unspoken things,
your world of pit shifts, battered down snap tins.

Torn apart by lonely headstock guillotines,
Billion Dollar slag heaps and greasepaint dreams.

Hymns About To Crash

"I still believe in God but God no longer believes in me."

Wayne Hussey

Amazing Graceland

The King of Rock 'n' Roll looks out across
the trailer park through antique
aviator shades.

Free of contracts, fat hypocrisies,
Graceland trinkets
deep fried excuses.

Allows his trademark quiff,
now white as the suits
he once wore, to shake gently
in the warm evening breeze.

Kids across the way yell out,
point fingers, call him creepy,
then try and remember where
they've seen that face before.

Elvis the Pelvis's hip replacements,
blue suede stranger in arthritic dance
Viva Las Vegas and bingo nights
Heartbreak Hotel
now an old folks home.

No more love me tenders,
or cabaret kisses,
Hollywood battles, conspiracy souls,
Suspicious Minds, Nixon sponsored
karate chopping entourage.

Later, he may pull out the jumpsuit
stand in front of the mirror
stare at old bones with painted sneer,

tarnished rhinestones
and ask himself *Are You Lonesome Tonight?*

The half recalled theme tune from *2001*
drums through hearing aid
via Tupelo, Mississippi
and daddy's tired Southern drawl

but that's not alright mama,
life going to hell quicker
than a sixpenny sick
seems the rest of the world can help
falling in love.

Everyone is managed
by their own private colonels – he understands that now.

But his ghosts are celluloid,
regrets of a million
terrible impersonators.

Sometimes when he saw
one of those old films
he cried.

Tonight though, he decides
they will only make him laugh.

So, what will he do now?
the King of Rock 'n' Roll
the twin that never was,
Memphis dream in a coronary.

Be satisfied with that bathroom demise?

Recite sideburn soliloquies
to long gone *Hula-Hula* girls?

No.

He will simply try to be.
Be what they would not allow.

There will be no more.

Return to Sender.

Elvis is leaving the building.

The world can stay where it is.

St Jude's

No one went there anymore,

cracked lead tiles, those not nicked,
hung loose above decayed,
moss encrusted brickwork.

Stained glass windows, years ago
had been used for target practice,
heads of biblical heroes shattered,
lost forever

to ancient ten bob kiddy bets.

On the notice board, over yellowed posters
for choir meetings and coffee mornings

no one went to

someone had sprayed the words

'GOD HELP US'.

The whole place cast a shadow
over the cemetery's pattern of crumbling ghosts,
headstones lost to weeds of time,
crisp bag, rubber johnny hauntings

If this had been a film, it would have been
called St Jude's, patron Saint of Lost Causes,
poetic license and all that,

the fact was no one even remembered
what it was called,

ignored it sulked there,
a gargoyle beast that never smiled.

Distant crooked shape on the horizon,

lone question mark

on a town's

slurred sentence.

Holy

They swap spittle kisses on unmade lips

let animal hands claw unworkable zips

in tangles of tights, wet-knicker blessings

saliva dipped bombs, hot tongues digressing

into hours of moments and thoughts of blood

pulsing predicaments in worlds beyond trust

mascara whispered, porcelain eyes

search for secrets to un-paint the sky.

After, they grasp for words not to say

an undressed silence exposes the day

they fall to each other, lost in gallows of dawn

in aching commandments,

forget they are born.

Cross Purposes

Stigmata bleeding hearts have stained
Damascus roads where *Volvos* park
by Eden's garden sprinkled realm,
temples lined with gravelled drives.

And lo, the water features spray
baptised lawns of idle talk,
cold indifferent *Avon* eyes
scan Gospels in the *Daily Mail*.

Lit fountains by the summerhouse
are fonts to dip gold fingers in,
anointed hands to bless each child
with private school place destiny.

Identical white fences form
a crucifixion barricade,
a sacrificial Judas kiss,
from curtain

twitching

promised lands.

Some Weird Sin

(Birmingham Hummingbird: 15 January 1991)

Iggy was beautiful, alien torso,
bohemian brutal, fucking the stage

rock 'n' roll carcass, cock in hands
lyrical murdering metal rage

sex-goth-terrorist, bastard savage,
primeval punk in leopard skin vest.

Bleached ragged *Levis*, scarlet flesh,
a smell of unattainable women and death.

Screaming horror, in turns of hate
an angry God sermon for children lost,

wrecked guitar, smeared in sweat
destruction riffs of filth and dogs.

Across the world at another gig
in smoked blown venue's search light beams

the music of the chopper blades
rips apart a country's seams

a crowd of rotten corpses don't
applaud the songs of armoured tanks

or thunder of the oil drums
or join in with the yankee dance

while Iggy mourns the underworld
and barks about the burning sands

mothers hold their kids and wait
for encore bombs in desert lands.

The first Iggy Pop gig I went to was at the Birmingham Hummingbird, it was the most brilliantly scary performance I have ever seen. The ex-Stooge, treating the live music stage as some sort of war zone carried more resonance the next day however, when after returning from the concert I discovered that the first Gulf War had started. Another war and more terrorist atrocities later, Iggy is still alive and well(?) – perhaps he can't be killed by conventional weapons.

Home

If there's no light
at the end of this tenner
I'll warm myself in your poverty,
lend myself to your bank of trust,
hand you broken bulbs of hope…

watch as you make them glow,
see artworks in the damp patches,
fairy tales in final warnings ,
peeling dreams of wallpaper love,
feel drafts of whispered
sweet regards.

Know this crumbling terrace
is our palace in the making,
know these missing tiles
are our windows onto heaven.

Know the rubbish telly
is a reason to go to bed with you,
know those tangled weeds outside
are flowers of romance.

Know the knackered heating
is why we cuddle up at night,
know that dripping tap
is the beating of a heart.

Know the siren rushing by
is music of the night,
a flashing blue lit overture,
a rhapsody of ravaged hymns.

If there's no light
at the end of this tenner
I'll warm myself in your poverty,
lend myself to your bank of trust,
hand you broken bulbs of hope…

ACKNOWLEDGEMENTS

Factory Space and *Now The Deer Have...* were previously published in *Under The Radar*.

Vostok 1 and *Sputnik II* were previously published in Andrew's Crystal Clear Creators pamphlet *Citizen Kaned*.